Original title:

The Pulse of the Islands

Copyright © 2025 Creative Arts Management OÜ
All rights reserved.

Author: Adeline Fairfax
ISBN HARDBACK: 978-1-80581-614-0
ISBN PAPERBACK: 978-1-80581-141-1
ISBN EBOOK: 978-1-80581-614-0

The Legacy of Roots and Winds

In a land where bananas wear hats,
And coconuts debate like chitchat,
Palm trees sway with a comical glee,
While fish in the sea share tea at three.

Frogs hop like they're in a dance show,
Laughter erupts as the winds blow,
Each blade of grass joins in the jest,
Nature calls out, 'Who can dance best?'

The sun wears sunglasses, cool as a cat,
While crabs throw a party, imagine that!
Seagulls squawk jokes like a stand-up king,
While waves clap hands, as the sea starts to sing.

Turtles race in a slow-motion race,
With shells decked out, each one a face.
The sand chuckles beneath playful toes,
In this paradise where laughter grows.

Rhythmic Embrace of Earth and Sea

A beach ball rolls, a seagull dives,
Shells laugh as they play with tides,
Crabs moonwalk, trying to impress,
As the horizon wears a sunset dress.

In the evening breeze, coconuts sway,
Whispers of secrets in a cheeky way,
Laughter echoes from wave to shore,
As the island wraps jokes in folklore.

Maracas rattle in the warm night air,
While starfish wear fedoras with flair,
The moon joins in with a giggle and glance,
Lighting the way for a carefree dance.

Under the palms, the laughter flows,
As the ocean tells tales that nobody knows,
With each little wave comes a punchline new,
In this playful realm, joy is the view.

Harmonies of Sunrise and Dusk

The rooster crows, it's morning time,
A fish sings out, it's quite a rhyme.
The sun stretches wide, yawning too,
While the trees dance in a morning dew.

At dusk, the crabs wear tiny hats,
As shadows play with sneaky bats.
The moon arrives with a smile so bright,
While the stars plan a party tonight.

Flickers of Fireflies at Twilight

In the garden, flickers dart and play,
Fireflies throw a glowing ballet.
They chat in code, lights on and off,
While frogs comment with a croak and scoff.

The night owl hoots, trying to trend,
But fireflies flash, he can't comprehend.
With soft giggles, they tease him so,
While crickets join in, putting on a show.

Nature's Symphony of Flora and Fauna

The flowers hum sweet tunes all day,
While bees dance in a buzzing ballet.
A little lizard tries to hit a note,
But his chipmunk buddy gives a hearty quote.

As the wind strums leaves like a guitar,
The parrots rap from near and far.
Together they form a quirky band,
Performing as nature's music stands.

Gentle Caress of the Trade Winds

The trade winds tickle the palm trees high,
As coconut husks roll by and sigh.
Seagulls gossip, flapping their wings,
While the ocean serenades with soft springs.

Shells play dress-up, all glitter and glam,
While crabs shuffle like they're part of a jam.
Together they sway, in harmony they twirl,
As the winds spin tales of this island whirl.

Enchanted Whispers of the Jungle

In the green where monkeys swing,
Frogs croak tunes, the vines do sing.
Laughter mingles with the breeze,
As parrots gossip from the trees.

Butterflies dance, they take a leap,
Caterpillars share secrets they keep.
Silly ants march in perfect line,
While sloths declare, 'We're doing fine!'

Resonance of Laughter and Traditions

Mangoes fall like sweet, ripe jokes,
Grandmas giggle with playful pokes.
Uncles dance with two left feet,
While kids scamper, oh what a feat!

Drums roll like thunder, feet in flight,
Laughter echoes through the night.
Fish tales told, tall as a tree,
While we feast on coconut spree.

Soliloquies by the Serene Stream

The stream chatters like old friends,
Where fish swim fast and laughter blends.
Frogs in chorus, a ribbit song,
As water nymphs join in along.

Breezes tease with breezy hair,
Nature giggles, it's quite the affair.
As ducks quack puns and boats do glide,
The stream whispers tales of pride.

Nature's Heartbeat Underneath

Beneath the grass, the critters play,
Squirrels chatter throughout the day.
Wiggly worms in their muddy beds,
Tickle the roots, laugh in their heads.

Bees buzz jokes as they gather round,
While daisies sway in jest profound.
Roots twist and twirl, they prance with glee,
Nature's laughter—a symphony!

The Beat of Island Drums

On the sands we dance and sway,
Drumsticks juggling, hippos play.
Scuttle crabs join in the fun,
Chasing shadows, all is one.

Fishermen trying to catch a fish,
But they only hook a mermaid's wish.
Laughter echoes down the shore,
As everyone yells, "We want more!"

Look! A pigeon in a hat,
Trying to catch a falling bat.
Turtles bopping with the beat,
Exchanging moves, it's quite the feat!

Oh, the island spirit soars high,
Even the parrot can make us sigh.
With each drumbeat, the smiles grow,
A crazy scene, what a show!

Echoes of Nature's Heart

The trees are gossiping, oh so loud,
While turtles wear a leafy shroud.
Birds in bandanas sing out tunes,
Underneath the laughing moons.

The ocean winks, a playful tease,
Tickling toes with a cool breeze.
Crabs throw a party in the surf,
Rolling and tumbling, chasing turf.

Jellyfish wear polka dots bright,
Floating around like balloons in flight.
Nature's echo, silly as can be,
Inviting all to join the spree!

And coconut drinks spill in delight,
Frothy laughter bubbling all night.
Funny is the rhythm here,
With each wave, we cheer, oh dear!

Serenade of the Shoreline

Starfish serenade the night,
With a seaweed band, what a sight!
Clams clap shells, creating a sound,
As waves splash and twirl around.

An octopus in a striped tie,
Trying to impress a seagull fly.
With each slip, he makes a splash,
The shoreline giggles with a crash.

Seashells whisper silly rhymes,
While dolphins dance to funny chimes.
The moon's reflection joins the cheer,
Swaying along to songs we hear.

What a melody of laughter and fun,
Underneath the warm, golden sun.
A shoreline ball, don't miss the scene,
Where goofy meets the ocean's sheen!

Whispers of Coconut Trees

Coconuts gossip, swaying slow,
Sharing tales of how they grow.
Birds drop by, in chatty array,
"Who stole my nut?!" they cry in dismay.

Palms wave hands like they know best,
Mistaking a squirrel for a guest.
With every breeze, a tickle's found,
In the laughter that goes round and round.

A toucan paints the sky with cheer,
While a gecko plays a ukulele here.
Lizards groove without a care,
As the sunburns a shirtless bear!

So gather 'round, the trees invite,
For every laugh, there's pure delight.
Nature's humor wraps us tight,
Under stars, we dance each night!

The Resonance of Island Dreams

Coconuts bounce like baseballs,
While fish wear tiny top hats.
Seagulls dance in flip-flops,
As crabs do their best at chitchat.

Palm trees gossip with the breeze,
Whispering secrets of old tunes.
Turtles glide with jokes to share,
Beneath the warmth of lazy moons.

The tide plays tag with sandy toes,
Shells wear grins like mischievous sprites.
Bananas hop, and pineapples joke,
In a land where laughter ignites.

Every sunset brings a belly laugh,
As the stars wink with playful glee.
Island dreams twirl in silly ways,
On waves of mirth—a comedy spree.

Flows of Forgotten Currents

Waves splash laughter on the shore,
Like kids splashing in puddles wide.
Seaweed floats singing folklore,
While dolphins giggle with pride.

The ocean wears a funny hat,
As jellyfish dance in odd shapes.
Crabs throw parties in a mat,
While seahorses take goofy drapes.

Sandcastles look like royal dens,
With towers made of silly cream.
And starfish hold hands with mermaids,
In a waterlogged, wild dream.

Tides tell tales that twist and turn,
With each new wave—an offbeat tune.
Laughter flows where currents churn,
In this whimsical, sandy boon.

Pulsing with Nature's Breath

Nature's heartbeat skips a beat,
As the wind wraps us in a hug.
Fluffy clouds stomp their happy feet,
While flowers grin, each one a thug.

The sun sneezes with a bright shine,
Tickling the leaves up in the trees.
Raindrops giggle down the vine,
Winking at all who catch the tease.

Leaves do the cha-cha in the breeze,
While frogs croak punchlines with a cheer.
Even ants join in with ease,
Dancing circles without a fear.

As moonlight looks on with delight,
Night critters hum a silly song.
In this pulsing rhythm of light,
Nature laughs, where we belong.

The Cadence of Coastal Dunes

Dunes sway like dancers in line,
Waves tap a beat that's just divine.
Seagrapes taste like sweetened dreams,
While sandpipers show off their gleams.

The horizon wears a playful grin,
As crabs practice their silly spins.
Beach umbrellas wave in the sun,
Bouncing like children having fun.

Tides tumble in a wacky race,
While sunsets paint the sky with grace.
Laughter hangs in salty air,
A serenade for those who dare.

Footprints lead to tales untold,
As laughter echoes, young and old.
In the rhythm of waves and sand,
There's magic in this playful land.

Tides Whispering Secrets

The waves gossip with the shore,
Telling tales of sunken lore.
A crab in a tux, quite a sight,
Bows to the fish, ready for a fight.

Seaweed dances, oh what a sight,
A fashion show at noon, so light!
Starfish claps in appreciation,
While seagulls plan their lunch vacation.

Vibrations of Coral Reefs

Beneath the waves, fish throw a ball,
Riding the currents, they're having a ball.
A parrotfish sings, a catchy new tune,
While an octopus plays peek-a-boo, too!

The sea turtles are joining the game,
With moves so slick, they're earning fame.
A clownfish laughs, in the coral he'll hide,
As his friend the eel, gets tangled and tied.

Melodies of Salt and Sand

On the beach, the seagulls croon,
As kids on the shore sway to the tune.
They build sandcastles, sans any pain,
Till the tide arrives, and claims their domain!

A sand crab shuffles with a little hat,
While the waves applaud, imagine that!
With shells as instruments, they join the beat,
Creating a concert, oh what a treat!

Lifeblood of the Ocean's Edge

Life at the shoreline, full of surprise,
A clam sells tickets, quite a disguise!
The jellyfish floats, with style and grace,
While sea urchins chuckle, in their prickly place.

The waves serve drinks, in coconut shells,
With mermaid bartenders ringing their bells.
Crabs in shades dance under the sun,
As all the sea critters join in for fun!

Rhythms of the Tides

The seaweed dances with a swish,
Crabs do the cha-cha, oh what a wish!
Fish flip-flop in synchronized time,
Seagulls audition for a seabird mime.

Sandcastles wobble, they breathe and sway,
Shells tell stories of yesterday's play.
Waves play peekaboo with the shore,
Collecting giggles, wanting more and more.

Turtles race, it's a slippery feat,
While old stingrays jitter on their fins so fleet.
Jellyfish twirl, naked and free,
They giggle at all the fun in the sea.

As sunset paints its colors so bright,
The whole beach parties under the light.
In this wacky dance of sea and land,
Joy is found, oh isn't life grand!

Heartbeat of the Ocean Breeze

Palm trees sway with a silly grin,
Blowing kisses to the waves akin.
Cockatoos chuckle as they fly,
While conch shells gossip with a sigh.

A coconut rolls; it starts to giggle,
A starfish watches with a little wiggle.
Winds play tag, spinning oh so fast,
Laughing at the shadows they cast.

The sun lays down for its golden nap,
While beach balls bounce in a hap-hap-hap.
Sandy toes doing the twist in style,
Every grain of sand boasts a multiple smile.

As night falls with its starry glow,
Stars wink at fish putting on a show.
In this breezy dance of light and fun,
The ocean laughs, it's never done!

Echoes from Shore to Shore

Shells echo tales of lazy days,
Of sun-kissed highs and jubilant rays.
Crabs boast loudly with big, brave hearts,
In this zany game of oceanic arts.

Tides tease turtles, 'Come try and race!'
While dolphins giggle, they set the pace.
Seashells collide with a clatter and clink,
The laughter grows, don't you think?

Waves whisper secrets to the grainy sand,
Tickling toes with a gentle hand.
Fishermen chuckle at their clever bait,
Their friendship with fish is something great.

As the moon pulls tides for one last cheer,
Barnacles shout, "We want our beer!"
In this funny echoing spree,
Every wave joins in, hearty and free!

Whispers of Tropical Winds

Tropical breezes with laughter ride,
Carrying secrets from the ocean wide.
Bananas giggle on their leafy trees,
While parakeets dance with goofy ease.

The wind tells jokes that only trees know,
Rustling leaves in a synchronized show.
Surfers crack up, wipeouts galore,
Bid farewell to dignity, it's quite the score!

Kites spiral up with a whoosh and a flail,
Chasing after clouds with a gusty wail.
Cocktails in hand, these winds celebrate,
Mixing up laughter on a grand plate.

Under starlit skies, the night's a riot,
Each breeze sings loud, it can't be quiet.
With each tickling gust, a hearty blend,
Life's a comedy, until the end!

Harmonies of Sand and Shell

On the shore, crabs all march,
In a line, they steal my lunch.
Seagulls cackle, doing their part,
While I'm left with crumbs to crunch.

Waves whisper secrets to the sand,
As I try to build a tower.
But a rogue wave, quick and grand,
Turns my castle into a shower!

Starfish gather for a buffet,
Eating sand, what a bold choice!
Jellyfish jive, throwing a sway,
Hoping to make the sea rejoice.

Laughter echoes from the shore,
Even fish are in on the joke.
With every splash, I ask for more,
Who knew sea life could provoke?

The Dance of the Moonlit Waves

Under the moon, fish start to prance,
Doing the cha-cha in the tide.
Octopuses join with a glance,
While jellyfish provide the glide.

Dancing shells twirl on the ground,
Whispering rhymes of the sea spray.
The mermaids giggle, all around,
As crabs tap dance, making hay.

Turtles bow with style and grace,
Winking at the sea cucumber.
It's a wild underwater race,
With conch shells sharing their slumber.

So grab your snorkel, come dig in,
In this ocean, fun does rule.
When the night ends, we all win,
Aerial fish form a cool pool!

Lullabies from the Palm Fronds

Palm trees sway with a lazy tune,
Breeze tickles them, they giggle back.
As coconuts fall like a cartoon,
I duck quick, avoiding the whack.

Lizards bask with a cheeky grin,
While toucans squawk jokes on the wire.
In this warm sun, all's a win,
Life here thrives with utmost fire.

Kids chase the shadows on the beach,
Building dreams where sandcastles stand.
But oh! A wave has them in reach,
Now they're heroes in the quicksand.

With palm fronds cradling our play,
Nature sings a silly song.
In every laugh, we find our way,
What could be better than this throng?

Songs of the Endless Blue

In the turquoise, fish wear hats,
Dancing in a sea of delight.
The sun broadcasts funny chats,
As dolphins leap, a comical sight.

Snorkels and flippers, a wild crew,
Racing to find a treasure chest.
But only found some seaweed stew,
I'd call it lunch, but it's not best!

Waves crash softly on the shore,
Spraying my toes in silly joy.
Every splash opens a door,
To playful moments we all enjoy.

So let the ocean sing its song,
Of bubbles, laughter, and good cheer.
In this vast blue, we all belong,
Each wave a tale, each wave a sneer!

Nature's Heartbeat Beneath the Stars

Crabs dance in the moonlight glow,
While fish throw a splash show.
The coconut trees sway and laugh,
As tourists take their sunbaked bath.

Waves crash like a drummer's beat,
A shell sings tunes we can't repeat.
Stars wiggle above in playful jest,
Nature's jokes are simply the best!

Fireflies flicker, a glowing gang,
They swarm the beach as the guitars twang.
The sea breeze whispers a giggling cheer,
As nightfall's humor draws us near.

In this realm of fun and bliss,
Every moan of wind feels like a kiss.
Under this laughing fabric spun,
We embrace, we frolic, we have our fun!

Tempest and Tranquility in Unity

A stormy sky wears a frown,
While waves play tag, up and down.
Raindrops bounce like children at play,
"Catch me if you can!" they say.

Inside a hut, we hear the roar,
Like nature's way of asking for more.
Lightning dances to a wild beat,
We sip our drinks, all cozy and sweet.

But soon the clouds give way to cheer,
The sun pops out, and we all shout "Dear!"
What a sight, the storm and sun,
A comedy act, just having fun.

With every breeze, the laughter soars,
As nature twirls, we crack up on shores.
In tempest's wake, tranquility's grace,
We embrace the wild, silly place!

Life's Overture on Sunlit Shores

The sun in the morn sings a loud tune,
As surfboards party, chasing the moon.
Seagulls audition for best comic flaps,
While kids build castles with epic mishaps.

Beach balls bounce like an errant boss,
Getting rolled over, oh what a loss!
Families giggle as they dodge the sprays,
While sandmen hold their goofy ways.

A picnic spread with all the fix,
But ants declared war, oh what a mix!
Laughter erupts, a banquet of bliss,
In the sunlit realm, we share a kiss.

Even the waves have a chuckling sound,
As they pull back treasures from underground.
An overture of joy plays every day,
On sunlit shores, where we laugh and play!

Echoes of the Ancient Land

Footsteps whisper of stories untold,
Beneath the sun, they alight like gold.
Ancient rocks chuckle with glee,
Remembering tales of you and me.

Turtles stroll, wearing wise old hats,
As pirates laugh, calling out to cats.
The breeze tells jokes of history lost,
As we wander, getting lost at all cost.

In the shadows, mysteries unfold,
Each laugh a memory wrapped in gold.
From mountain high to ocean low,
The land is alive with a chuckling flow.

Echoes resound in this merry place,
With every step, we share a space.
In the ancient land's charm so grand,
Life's ebbs and flows, a humorous band!

Symphony of Celestial Skies

When stars play hide and seek at night,
The crabs hold a concert, oh what a sight!
Seagulls sing out their off-key tune,
While fish dance under the laughing moon.

A dog barks loudly—it's joined the fun,
With a leap and a wag, it races the sun.
Turtles, in slow-mo, groove on the sand,
Shuffling along with a beach ball in hand.

The waves throw a party, what a big splash,
As surfers wobble in an awkward dash.
Jellyfish spin in their jelly-like way,
Chasing bright shadows that playfully sway.

So let's join the dance, with a skip and a hop,
In this wacky world, we'll never stop.
With laughter that echoes, we'll soar on high,
Under the jolly glow of the island sky.

Murmurs of Serene Lagoons

In a lagoon where the fish wear hats,
A turtle jests with the gossiping rats.
The breeze whispers jokes through the palm trees,
While the crickets chirp with the greatest of ease.

Frogs on lily pads make quite the scene,
Croaking their tales, oh what a routine!
The water's a stage for this lively crew,
Where the ducklings waddle, in boots made of goo.

A crab in a tux leads a dance with flair,
As the algae sway, without a single care.
The sun yawns big, stretching up from the bay,
And the ghostly moon chuckles, "Not yet, I say!"

Here's to the antics that float on the breeze,
For in quiet lagoons, it's all just a tease.
With giggles and splashes, we won't be discreet,
In this watery world, life's always a treat.

The Beat of the Coral Reef

Down in the reef where the fish love to joke,
A parrotfish cracks up with a bob and a poke.
The sea anemones sway to their beat,
As clownfish giggle with floppy little feet.

A conch shell shouts, "Hey, listen to me!"
While the octopus swirls in a dance with glee.
Sea turtles chuckle, as they take their time,
Moving in rhythm, like a silly mime.

The sea cucumbers chill with no fear,
While the sea fans flutter, spreading good cheer.
Starfish wiggle in their five-armed glee,
Calling out, "Join in! It's party time, whee!"

So let's ride the waves of this colorful scene,
With laughter and jests, we'll reign as the queen.
In the heart of the ocean, this joy we'll keep,
As the coral reef sings us into a leap.

Enchanting Currents: A Love Song

In the currents where mermaids twirl and swirl,
A fish fell in love with a bright seashell girl.
With a wink and a flip, he tried to impress,
But tripped on a seaweed, causing a mess.

Starry-eyed, the shells giggled and peeped,
As the clownfish chuckled, their secrets they'd keep.
Then up came a lobster, with big claws held wide,
Saying, "Love's like seaweed, it grows on the tide!"

A dolphin chimed in with a flip of his tail,
"Love's not just smooth, it can also derail!"
As bubbles erupted, they laughed and they swayed,
In this underwater waltz, no one's dismayed.

With each splash and swirl, they danced through the sea,
In a love song so funny, all wild and free.
So here's to the currents, with laughter they bring,
In the depths of the ocean, let your heart sing!

Currents of Time and Tradition

The fish dance lightly, oh what a sight,
In the market, they twirl, taking flight.
Old tales are told with a wink and a grin,
As coconut drinks spill, we all dive in.

The grandmothers gossip while sipping their tea,
What's the latest scandal? Oh, let's see!
They throw in a jiggle, a laugh, and a nudge,
As the crowd joins in, no sign of a grudge.

The roosters crow loudly, they think they're the stars,
They strut through the streets with no worries or scars.
While the tourists just chuckle, they cluck right back,
In a world of pure chaos, we rejoice in the lack.

With drums that go boom and a rhythm so sweet,
We dance till we drop, stumbling on our feet.
Time wobbles by like a hammock in breeze,
In the heart of tradition, we laugh with such ease.

Starlit Skies and Gentle Laughs

Under the stars, we sway to the tune,
While the crickets sing softly, they're quite the boon.
With fireflies glowing, we're lost in the night,
And laughter erupts as we trip in delight.

The moon's our spotlight, it shines on our mess,
Each flip and each fall draws the crowd to confess.
We play charades, and the winner's a mime,
But the jokes turn to giggles, our hearts feel sublime.

The breeze brings the scent of sweet pineapple dreams,
As slip-ups ensue, we're bursting at the seams.
A splash from a wave leads to joyful shrieks,
In this comedy show, we're all little peaks.

So let's toast to the night with our cups held high,
To the sparkles and giggles, the stars in the sky.
For laughter's the treasure in this joyful land,
Beneath starlit skies, we'll dance hand in hand.

Flavors of Paradise in Every Bite

Oh, the feast awaits with a colorful spread,
Tropical treats that dance in your head.
The mango is sweet, the breadfruit delights,
But beware of the spice that ignites wild fights.

Crispy fish tacos, they simply can't wait,
While the island's delight brings a taste of fate.
We gobble and chuckle as sauces collide,
And if meals were a swim, we'd all just slide!

Pudding's a mystery, what flavor is that?
Coconut, tamarind, or a chocolate chat?
We nibble with glee, for this is our bliss,
In the festival of flavors, we steal each sweet kiss.

So join in the laughter, come taste and explore,
With every new dish, we giggle for more.
In this land of abundance, we savor the fun,
A culinary dance where the jokes never run.

Ocean Mist Kissing Island Dreams

The ocean breeze giggles, a tickle on toes,
As crab pots bob gently, they're putting on shows.
Beneath the cool waves, the fish laugh and play,
While we join in, splashing, no worries today.

The sandcastles tumble, the kids squeal with glee,
As seagulls drop fries just for you and for me.
We juggle our snacks with a wink and a grin,
Landing right in the surf, where the fun will begin.

With shells as our treasures, we search for the best,
And a hermit crab scuttles, it's quite the jest.
We watch as it dances, all awkward and shy,
And we laugh 'till we ache, under the wide, sunny sky.

So let's raise a toast with coconut milk,
To the waves and the laughter, as smooth as fine silk.
With ocean mist swirling, our dreams drift and play,
In this land of mischief, we're happy to stay.

Island Vibrations through Timeless Seasons

The sun shines bright, a golden tease,
Seagulls squawk like they're having a breeze.
Turtles in shades of lime and brown,
Dance on the shore, never wearing a frown.

Coconuts dropping with humorous plop,
They roll like they know they can't stop.
Palm fronds wave in a playful jest,
Who knew nature could party so best?

The waves tickle toes, a seaweed tick,
Fish sport sunglasses, doing their trick.
Sandcastles grow like dreams in the sun,
Even the crabs join in on the fun!

Seasons shift, yet laughter remains,
Whimsical tunes from the old rusty chains.
Island life spins in a merry whirl,
Under the stars, let the laughter unfurl.

Swaying Songs of Windswept Trees

Trees chuckle softly in the warm sea air,
With branches that tickle, they giggle and share.
Roots intertwined like friends in a dance,
Each leaf a laughter, a flutter, a chance.

The wind whispers jokes, rustling leaves just right,
As branches sway low in a playful sight.
Nature's own choir sings "Here Comes the Fun!"
Each note a splatter of sunshine and run!

A toucan chuckles, bright beak all aglow,
Swinging on vines, putting on a show.
Lizards in hats, strutting with flair,
With each jump and leap, they're debonair.

Cool shadows play tag as the sun dips low,
Join in the laughter, let your worries go.
Leaves dance to rhythms, in sync with the breeze,
Tales of the trees echo through the seas.

Nature's Embrace in Every Breath

The ocean's breath tickles salty skin,
Laughs of the seashore, where fun begins.
Clouds float like cotton, gentle and meek,
They wink at the sun with a playful sneak.

Bananas in hammocks swinging with glee,
Say, "Life is sweet, come lounge with me!"
Fishes in masks, they swim without care,
Bubbles of giggles burst into the air.

A crab in a race, oh what a sight,
Pinching the shorts of a nearby kite.
Every wave tells a riddle or two,
As laughter ripples, both silly and true.

Tropical scents float on the breeze,
Mixing with joy and the taste of tease.
Nature's embrace wrapped in humor and cheer,
Each playful moment, a treasure held dear.

Living Dreams in a Tropical Oasis

Under palm trees, a hammock swings slow,
Sipping coconut juice, putting on a show.
The breeze plays tricks, sways hats away,
While everyone giggles, on this sunny day.

Flamingos in pink, striking poses galore,
Practicing runway walks, who could ask for more?
A monkey steals chips, how cheeky indeed,
While others just laugh, that's all they need.

Sunsets paint skies, colors wild and bright,
As fireflies twinkle, marking the night.
Each star a giggle, twinkling so free,
In this dream-like embrace, come laugh with me.

Living dreams here, where joy knows no bounds,
The ocean hums softly, in magical sounds.
An oasis of laughter, where troubles take flight,
We dance in the starlight, oh what a night!

The Rhythm of Vibrant Flora.

In gardens where the parrots dance,
The flowers throw a wild romance.
Petals wearing polka dots,
Even cacti spin in colorful spots.

With every bloom, a laugh's unfurled,
As bees waltz in a buzzing world.
Buds that tease with fragrant air,
Like flirty friends who often share.

The ferns do a jig, quite a sight,
While orchids flirt with morning light.
Sunflowers turn their heads to tease,
"Come join the party!" they seem to breeze.

So raise a cup of coconut milk,
And toast the color, sweet as silk.
For nature's fun, we're on this ride,
In every hue, laughter won't hide.

Rhythms of Lapping Waves

The ocean's laughter rolls ashore,
With splashes bright, it shouts for more.
Seagulls join in, a honking crew,
As surfboards dance like they're brand new.

In the sun, a crab tries to prance,
While shells join in for a daring chance.
"Catch me if you can!" each tide does say,
As fish throw parties, making waves play.

Surfboards bobbing with silly grace,
Waves tickle toes in a frothy race.
Paddleboarders grin, they can't believe,
How much fun the ocean can weave!

So let the waters giggle and splash,
With each wave, we'll let out a laugh.
In rhythm with the tide's sweet calls,
Let's ride the joy as each wave falls.

Echoes in the Tropical Breeze

The wind whispers tales, a playful tease,
It carries giggles through the trees.
Palm fronds sway, they can't stay still,
Like gossiping friends with time to kill.

The coconuts chuckle high above,
As fruit flies waltz, oh how they love!
While breezes sneak, tickling your ear,
"Chase us, chase us! We're always near!"

Even the lizards skitter and slide,
Joining the fun, they feel the tide.
"Catch us if you can!" they cheer and shout,
In the laughter of trees, there's no doubt.

So let's run with the wind, let it guide,
Where nature and giggles blend side by side.
In echoes of joy as they tease the leaves,
The breeze will lift your worries and reprieves.

Heartbeats Beneath the Palms

Beneath the palms, the shadows play,
Where laughter hides and runs away.
The squirrels race with nutty cheer,
While sunburnt tourists lend their ear.

The coconuts drop with a comical thud,
"Watch out!" they say, spilling sweet floods.
The beach dogs dig like there's no tomorrow,
Laughing with seashells, sound a bit hollow!

In the hush of noon, come antics galore,
Where sunbathers nap, then rise with a roar.
The local kids play a game of catch,
While the crabs step sideways, not quite a match.

So take a moment, let laughter in,
Join the party where smiles begin.
For beneath the palms, the heartbeats thrum,
In the dance of the day, let's all be dumb!

Currents of Tide and Time

The waves go up, they come back down,
Frogs in tuxedos, hopping around.
Windy hats soar, like sailboats in flight,
As seagulls argue, it's quite the sight.

Shells hold secrets, gossip so sweet,
Crabs moonwalk, tapping their feet.
Fish throw parties, a splashy affair,
While turtles glide without a care.

Sandcastles topple in a loud cheer,
Sunscreen battles, we all hold dear.
Surfboards zipping, like snacks on the go,
Who knew the tide had such a show?

Balloons pop with a rip-roaring tune,
Chasing beach balls under the moon.
With every wave, laughter does bloom,
In this seaside circus, it's fun that we zoom.

Cascades of Laughter and Waves

A splash from a dolphin, what a prank!
He steals my sandwich, oh, that cheeky prank!
Seashells giggle, as crabs march group,
While seaweed dances, leading the troop.

The sun's a joker, flickering bright,
Playing tag with clouds, oh what a sight!
Flip-flops fling, they leap and they fly,
As gulls trade jokes with a wink of an eye.

Driftwood statues, posing all day,
Shells tell tales in their own twisted way.
The ocean whispers, "Catch a good wave!"
With laughter and joy, we're all so brave.

To crabs it's a dance, to fish, a parade,
What's serious here? It's all just a charade!
Under bright umbrellas, chatter so loud,
In this watery world, we all feel proud.

Sunsets Singing to the Stars

The sun dips low, a silly clown,
Pinking the sky in a vibrant gown.
Stars peek out, in pajamas they stare,
As night teases day with a playful dare.

Fireflies sparkle, like snacks in the air,
Whispers of dreams float without a care.
The moon cracks jokes with a laugh so bright,
As shadows join in for a song each night.

Waves join the chorus with splashes of cheer,
While the crickets hum, their tune so near.
Balloons drift up, on a chase with the breeze,
As laughter echoes through rustling leaves.

Twinkle, twinkle, oh what a night!
With giggles and grins, everything's right.
In this grand show of cosmic ballet,
We dance on dreams until break of day.

Festival of Colors in the Breeze

Colors are splashed like painted delight,
Kites flirt and giggle, floating in sight.
The sun throws confetti, all golden and bright,
While breadfruit dances, what a funny sight!

Shimmery shells in a wild masquerade,
As palmtrees sway in their own charade.
The sea whispers secrets that tickle the toes,
As friendship blooms where the warm wind blows.

Mangoes, bananas, oh sweet carnival,
Prancing about, having a ball.
Laughter bounces off waves in a spree,
With drums and maracas, we join in the glee!

Under the stars, the whole world comes alive,
With hues like candy, we twist and we jive.
As laughter cascades in joyous release,
In this vibrant fiesta, we savor the peace.

A Dance of Breath and Water

In a land where the palm trees sway,
The crabs do a jig at the end of the day.
With waves like a band, the sea joins in,
As the fish practice their mermaid grins.

A dolphin slips by with a comedic twist,
He waves with a fin, you just can't resist.
The turtles doze off, in their shells they snore,
While seagulls perform, the best show on shore.

Laughter floats through the salty breeze,
As I attempt to dance, just to feel at ease.
The splashes sound like the best of tunes,
As I trip on a wave, beneath the light of moons.

So if you feel blue when the skies turn gray,
Just grab a seashell, and dive in the spray.
A dance with the water, so joyful and free,
Join the party, oh come, it's just you and me!

Serenading the Shore with Moonlight

Under the moon, the crickets play,
The shore comes alive to a fun cabaret.
With coconuts clapping, a rhythm so sweet,
Even the sand crabs get up on their feet.

The waves hum a tune as they crash on the sand,
While the stars throw their glitters, all carefully planned.
But watch out for the seagulls with feathers askew,
They swoop for a snack; don't take it from you!

A conch sings a ballad, its voice all aglow,
But hey, did it just rhyme? Well, I guess it's a show!
The moon chuckles down, casting shadows so wide,
As we shimmy and shake with charm as our guide.

So grab your flip-flops, let's dance through the night,
With laughter and joy, oh, it feels so right.
The shore serenades with its lively delight,
In this waltz of the ocean, we'll never lose sight!

Reflections in the Lagoon's Embrace

In a lagoon where the lilies bloom,
The frogs hold a meeting, discussing their gloom.
They croak about flies and the hops that they missed,
While the fish laugh aloud, quite enjoying the gist.

A funny old turtle floats by with a style,
He sports a tall hat, oh, that's quite a mile!
His pals all chuckle, but he just winks back,
In this world of oddities, there's nothing quite slack.

As the breeze whispers sweet with a tickle of dew,
The dragonflies dance, causing quite a hullabaloo.
Reflections ripple, amused by the sight,
While everyone snickers at this playful light.

So come take a dip in this comedic retreat,
Where humor and nature so joyfully meet.
In this embrace of the lagoon's merry cheer,
Your worries will fade; it's laughter you'll hear!

Shimmering Sand and Solitude

On a stretch of sand where the sunbeams fall,
I tried building castles, but they weren't so tall.
The waves kept laughing, washing them away,
While I pondered if it was the sand or my play.

With my bucket in hand, I set off on a quest,
To find the best seashell, oh that would be the best!
But the crabs hoard treasures; they're crafty indeed,
I swear I saw one with a shimmery bead.

A lone coconut rolls by, giggling with glee,
That rascal's got jokes! What else could it be?
As seagulls debate my rightful claim,
Their raucous feud puts my efforts to shame.

Yet solitude dances in this sunny delight,
With each grain of sand, a soft laugh takes flight.
For in the humor of nature, I find my space,
Among shimmering sand, I embrace the warm grace!

The Dance of Light on Waves

Bubbles dance and twirl with glee,
As fish wear hats and join the spree.
The sun takes a dive, splashing bright,
While crabs do the cha-cha, what a sight!

Seagulls squawk with perfect timing,
Telling jokes that are quite sublime-ing.
A dolphin leaps, does a backflip too,
While wave-riding turtles look for a brew!

The shore is alive with laughter and cheer,
Even the sandcastles add a new ear!
They wave their turrets and giggle in sand,
As the ocean embraces the joy of the land.

Rising Sun and Singing Winds

The rooster crows with a funky twist,
While island folks can't help but twist!
The sun yawns wide, shakes off the night,
And the palm trees sway, feeling just right.

Coconuts giggle in the morning light,
As kites fly higher, what a sight!
The breeze whistles tunes both loud and high,
It's a day for dancing, oh me, oh my!

Hammocks swing like a merry-go-round,
While smiling clams mock the lazy hound.
The waves crash in, bringing laughter anew,
With a splash of fun, and maybe a brew!

Chasing Echoes of Island Legends

Ghost crabs scuttle with a riddle or two,
While a turtle tells tales of ocean blue.
The wave whispers softly, a secret revealed,
In the lullabies sung by the seaweed field.

Mermen play chess, with shells as their pieces,
While starfish argue in their own little leases.
The air is thick with tales and jest,
A frog stands up, claiming he's best!

Laughter erupts as the tales unfold,
Of mermaids who pranked, of treasures untold.
The sun rolls its eyes as tales go astray,
While crickets and lizards join in the play!

Vivid Dreams in a Coral Kingdom

Deep in the reefs, where colors collide,
The fishes wear smiles, like they've nothing to hide.
An octopus juggles, while sea fans applaud,
In a kingdom of laughter, where joyous dreams trod.

The seahorses prance, looking dapper and neat,
While eels share secrets, tapping their feet.
The jellyfish glide, like bubbles of joy,
In a world so bright, they can't be coy.

Coral castles pop in a carnival hue,
As snails run a race, in a snail-paced queue.
The tides are a rhythm, a dance of delight,
In this underwater party, everything feels right!

The Symphony of Dusk and Dawn

Seagulls squawk while I sip my drink,
A sunset hue makes the dolphins wink.
The crab's doing the conga on the shore,
And the starfish sings "Encore! Encore!"

The breeze tickles my nose, it's a funny sight,
As turtles juggle shells, oh what a delight!
Even the palm trees sway to the beat,
In this concert of quirks, life's hard to beat.

Glowworms twinkle, and fireflies dance,
The moon starts to hum; it's a wild romance.
Ah, the night wears laughter, its gown full of stars,
While a crab in a tuxedo strums on guitars.

As dawn peeks through, the giggles don't cease,
With coffee-stained mugs and a side of peace.
The world awakes with a cheer and a clap,
What fun in a world that's a silly mishap!

Harmonizing with Ocean's Caress

A clam and a whale had a karaoke night,
They sang 'Under the Sea' till the morning light.
A starfish played bass with eight arms on the go,
While the jellyfish glowed, stealing the show.

The octopus juggled with nautical flair,
Telling two fish jokes, they gasped for air.
A dolphin tossed beach balls, oh what a sight,
As a pelican swooped in and joined the slight.

Surfboards are dancing on the crest of a wave,
While crabs do the moonwalk, oh how they rave!
Seashells are clapping, the ocean's a stage,
With laughter and bubbles, it's all the rage.

As twilight arrives, the coral ensemble,
With a punchline so big, even sharks start to tremble.
Under stars that chuckle, with giggles so sweet,
We harmonize nicely, a funny retreat!

The Song of Endless Horizons

On a boat made of laughter, we sail the vast blue,
With a parrot that squawks, "Pineapple stew!"
The wind whispers jokes through the swaying sails,
While fish wear sunglasses and tell fishy tales.

With every horizon, more giggles arise,
A mermaid next door checks her seaweed ties.
She strums on a conch, a tune so absurd,
While the octopus dances, it's truly unheard.

Each wave brings a chuckle, each splash, a delight,
As the sun plays peekaboo, day turns to night.
The horizons are endless, the fun never stops,
With sea cucumbers lining up for the props.

So let's sail through the laughter, explore every joke,
With bubbles of humor in every stroke.
The ocean sings brightly, its symphony sweet,
In a world filled with whimsy, our quirks can't be beat!

Tides of Time and Memory

The tide tickles toes, as it dances ashore,
Little treasures of driftwood and shells to explore.
We build silly castles, they teeter, they sway,
While seagulls conspire, taking snacks away.

An old man whispers tales of the waves long ago,
His beard's a map of laughs, with a twinkle to show.
A memory's born with each hearty wave,
In the sands of our time, a treasure we crave.

The sunsets are wild, like a painter gone mad,
With colors so vibrant, it makes the crabs glad.
They moonwalk through puddles, with sassy aplomb,
Creating a rhythm, oh so full of charm.

As night falls around, in a blanket of stars,
The ocean shares secrets, like candlelit bars.
With laughter and love in the tide's gentle flow,
We dance through our memories, just letting it go!

Rhythmic Sway of Hibiscus

In the breeze, the flowers peep,
With every sway, they giggle deep.
A little bee lost in the dance,
Thinks he's got a grand romance.

Palm trees sway with playful grace,
Bowing low in a delightful race.
The coconuts fall with quite a thunk,
As if the trees had too much funk.

Lizards pose on a sunlit rock,
Giving side-eye like a comedy shock.
With tiny feet, they steal the scene,
Claiming the crown of royalty keen.

Nature throws a party, oh so bright,
With each wave crashing, pure delight.
We laugh and twirl, no signs of stress,
In this wild island happiness.

Luminous Skies and Seafoam Dreams

Under skies that play peek-a-boo,
A duck floats by in a tiny canoe.
With a quack and a splash, he sets the tone,
Making waves like he's never alone.

The sun beams down with a wink and a grin,
As crabs do a dance, their own little spin.
Shells wave their flags, a colorful crew,
Join in the fun, it's all good as new!

Fish wearing shades swim past the shore,
Demanding attention, they want an encore.
With bubbles that giggle and fins that twirl,
They invite us all to join their whirl.

As night falls, the stars play cards,
Laughing at clouds and playing their guards.
In dreams of foam, we dance with glee,
In a world where laughter is always free.

Celestial Dances in Island Air

The moon wears a hat made of bright rays,
Dancing with stars in the softest of plays.
A crab in a tux steps on stage,
Bow ties and all—oh, what a sage!

Fronds flutter like they've had too much juice,
Chasing each other, a green-haired truce.
The night air hums a merry tune,
Inviting all of us to croon.

With clouds like cotton candy so sweet,
The island's nightlife can't be beat.
They tip a wink as the waves take flight,
Bringing joy to every soul tonight.

And in this dream, we sway and prance,
Content to embrace each merry chance.
Island life, a whimsical affair,
Where laughter sparkles in the salty air.

Heartstrings Through Lush Canopies

Beneath the trees, a loud laugh rings,
As squirrels borrow hats fit for kings.
They chat away, plotting a scheme,
To steal a snack or live the dream.

Parrots gossip with flair and style,
Painting the air with colors that smile.
Each feathered friend has tales to share,
Of outings and shenanigans beyond compare.

The breeze rustles leaves, like whispers of fun,
Tickling branches, making them run.
A chameleon grins with a colorful twist,
And proclaims himself the star of the list.

In this canvas of green, we frolic, we play,
Creating memories that brightened our day.
Where joy is a song sung under the trees,
And laughter dances upon every breeze.

Vibrant Life in Every Particle

In a coconut shell, I found a cat,
Doing yoga on a mat, oh fancy that!
Lizards gossiping under the hot sun,
Joking with palms, just having fun.

Fish in the water with a flair for style,
Wearing tiny hats, they swim a mile.
Seagulls playing poker on the sand,
Calling out bids, isn't life just grand?

A crab in a tux, strutting by the shore,
Claiming he's rich and looking for more.
Turtles in shades with a beach towel spread,
Throwing a party, "Don't let fun be dead!"

So join the revelry, dance in the tide,
Life's a bit silly, come take a ride.
In every splash, a joke to be found,
Laughter and joy, all around is sound.

Warmth in the Breath of the Ocean

The waves whispered secrets, hilariously grand,
As surfers tried to stand, but fell like a band.
Sea turtles laughed at their clumsy grand scheme,
Floating like clouds in a daytime dream.

The sun wore glasses, a playful display,
While crabs hosted beach frisbee all day.
Seashells giggled, tucked in the foam,
"Sandy you're funny, just like our home!"

A mermaid in flip-flops, her hair in a bun,
Said "Can you pass me my sunscreen? Oh, what fun!"
Starfish applauded with a wave of each arm,
As the sea breeze embraced with such playful charm.

A hammock swung low, cradling a seashell,
Whispering tales of the sea's funny spell.
Join in the laughter, let your worries float,
In this quirky haven, joy's the antidote.

Tidal Rhythms and Quiet Dreams

At sunrise, the beach hosts a jovial choir,
With crabs on maracas, they never tire.
The tide rolls in with a squish and a slop,
While sea urchins wiggle, they just can't stop.

A dolphin in shades does the limbo with ease,
As seagulls watch on, giggling in the breeze.
The jellyfish glide, all dressed in fine robes,
Holding a cotillion, spreading fun globes.

A pufferfish joked, "This water's too warm!"
While octopuses danced, oh such a charm!
With each wave's pulse, there's laughter abound,
In these tidal rhythms, joy is renowned.

Dreams float like bubbles, bursting with cheer,
With playful reflections that tickle the ear.
The ocean sings softly, a sweet serenade,
In the heart of the waves, where worries fade.

Carried by the Wind's Embrace

The breeze tells stories that tickle and tease,
Of seagulls in capes flying high with such ease.
Whispers like bubbles that pop with a flash,
"Surfboards or kites? Let's have a splash!"

The palm trees chuckle, swaying in sync,
Throwing shade for beachcombers who wink.
A crab in a bow tie offers a toast,
"To the funniest fish, let's celebrate most!"

Kites dance above, in a colorful swirl,
While sandcastles giggle, each turret a twirl.
Wind spins the tales that bring joy to the day,
As the ocean dips low, in a whimsical sway.

So let's chase the breeze, with laughter in tow,
For the secrets it carries are fun, don't you know?
In the heart of the islands, we find our delight,
With humor and joy, every day feels just right.

Kaleidoscope Views of Distant Horizons

In the sky, colors twist and twirl,
Fish wear hats and dance with a whirl.
Palm trees gossip, swaying with glee,
While crabs tell jokes to the bumblebee.

Sunset paints the world with a grin,
Seagulls argue on where to begin.
Sandy castles laugh as they tumble down,
Even the waves seem to wear a crown.

Islanders shimmy, and shake with flair,
While coconuts join in the wild affair.
Shells play music, some strange, some sweet,
As frogs in bow ties tap their little feet.

Laughter stretches, a brightening kite,
While fish in tuxedos take off in flight.
In this fanciful place where giggles bloom,
Life's a sweet party that's bursting with zoom!

Threads of Life Woven by the Sea

The octopus knits with sun-kissed yarn,
Sea turtles model the latest in charm.
Starfish audition as twinkling baubles,
Creating laughter amid ocean squabbles.

Waves skip like children, laughing along,
As dolphins play tag in a bubbly song.
Anemones wiggle, wearing bright hats,
While crabs strut sideways like fashionable cats.

In a raft made of seaweed, a party's in swing,
With mermaids chuckling, they each take a fling.
The moon peeks down, winking with glee,
"Let's all get together; join in with me!"

Threads of life dance, entwined in the foam,
While fish in tuxedos find their sweet home.
Laughter floats high, carried on breezy air,
In this dazzling place, we find joy everywhere!

Secrets Held in Tropical Shadows

In the coconut grove, secrets abound,
Lizards in sunglasses lounge on the ground.
The whispers of palms tell tales of delight,
While raccoons in capes venture out for a bite.

Bamboo shoots giggle, tickling the breeze,
As hermit crabs trade shells with pretended ease.
Secretive parrots squawk riddles and rhymes,
Sharing glaring gossip while sipping on limes.

Magical shadows dance in twilight hues,
Where iguanas wear slippers, the world to amuse.
Cactus throws parties for owls dressed in style,
While crabs play charades, all grinning the while.

Under the stars, they share funny quirks,
From mermaid melodies to pixie perks.
In the hush of the night, laughter spills and flows,
In these tropical nooks, where sheer joy grows!

Crystalline Waters and Golden Shores

On golden sands, the sunbeams bounce,
While jellyfish glide, doing their pounce.
In crystalline waters, laughter erupts,
As playful fish join in, swirling in flups!

Seashells giggle, each with a tale,
Of pirates and treasure, and great windy sail.
Turtles wear sneakers, dashing with flair,
While crabs play a game of who can compare.

The breeze carries chuckles, tickling our ears,
As dolphins share secrets of past sunny years.
Under the sun, everyone's a comedian,
With jokes that flow like a jovial median.

As sun sets low, a glow fills the sky,
Each wave whispers jokes to the moon hanging high.
With hearts intertwined and laughter in store,
In this whimsical haven, we keep wanting more!

Nature's Serenade of Resilience

In tangled vines, a goat so free,
Spins tales beneath the coconut tree.
Laughter echoes through the breeze,
While a crab dances with a bee.

The waves, they chuckle, soft and light,
As a fish tells secrets out of sight.
The parrot squawks, a joke on cue,
While a turtle claims, 'I'm faster than you!'

Under bright suns, all creatures play,
With rhythms that make the day sway.
From palm to sand, a chorus rings,
Nature's joy in the dance it brings.

So let the sun set on this spree,
With wild laughs and vibrant glee.
In every rustle, a story told,
Of humor found in nature's fold.

Nuances of Night and Day in Paradise

As dusk descends, the crickets cheer,
Their evening song, a nightly beer.
The moon gives winks, a sly delight,
While shadows stretch, preparing for flight.

Sleepy owls wear their fuzzy hats,
While roosters dream of morning chats.
The stars compete in shiny crowns,
As night reveals its silly gowns.

At dawn, the sun pranks with bright rays,
Waking all in a playful daze.
The monkeys hoot, a breakfast call,
While gulls dive down for a fishball.

In this dance of night and day,
Each hour has jokes it wants to play.
A cycle spun in laughter's glow,
Paradise hums with joy in tow.

Whirlwinds of Flora and Fauna

A flamboyant flower, in colors grand,
Dances with wind, it can't quite stand.
A cheeky butterfly flirts on by,
While bamboo groves giggle, oh my!

Vines twist like ribbons in a race,
While roots whisper secrets, with grace.
A squirrel drops an acorn down,
It's nature's messenger, wearing a crown.

Lizards strut in their flashy scales,
While frogs croak out their wild tales.
As blossoms bloom, the bees conspire,
In this whirlwind of life, they never tire.

With each breeze, there's a chuckle bright,
As flora and fauna delight in flight.
Together they spin, in joy and glee,
Nature's circus, wild and free.

Islands Resonating with Heritage

From stones and shells, stories unfold,
Of ancient lives, both brave and bold.
As drums beat rhythms from the past,
Echoes of laughter, forever cast.

In colorful markets, the vendors shout,
Bartering goods with a joyful rout.
Fisherman grins with a catch so neat,
While the parrot squawks, 'A deal, so sweet!'

Dances swirl under the moonlit skies,
With traditional moves that mesmerize.
Grandma spins tales of yesteryears,
As laughter mingles with joyful cheers.

In this melting pot of tales and song,
Heritage weaves where all belong.
Islands alive with spirit and cheer,
A humor-filled past, forever dear.

Embracing the Spirit of the Waters

In the water where we splash,
Fish swim by with quite a dash.
We dive down to catch a wink,
Oh wait, that's just my drink!

The waves come in and start to play,
Surfboards float and sway all day.
I tried to ride, but slipped and fell,
Now all the crabs I know can tell!

Seagulls laugh and steal my fries,
They've got those sneaky, greedy eyes.
I'll simply wave, my snack now lost,
It seems they're having quite the toss!

The sun sets down like a glowing gem,
My friends and I sing just for them.
Yet one fell in, with a giant splash,
Now we all laugh—oh what a crash!

Shores of Wonder and Discovery

I found a shell, so pink and bright,
I thought it'd make a great delight.
But when I held it to my ear,
It whispered, 'Hey, get out of here!'

A crab was hiding, just my luck,
It pinched my toe, oh what a pluck!
I danced around, not one bit shy,
As beachgoers giggled, passing by.

The sunbathers sunbathe, all serene,
But I'm more of the water scene.
I cannonball, a splash so fun,
My sunscreen? Well, it's now just gone!

Treasures are found where laughter rings,
Little joys in small, silly things.
With sand in toes and hearts so free,
We sing and dance, just you and me!

Footprints in Time Beneath the Stars

Under the moon, we dance and sway,
With glow sticks shining through the spray.
But then I tripped and fell face-first,
A bruise? No! Just a sparkling burst!

Footprints in sand tell tales so grand,
Of silly pranks and a lost flip-flop band.
We draw our names, all wobbly and wide,
And giggle at how the tide can slide!

The stars above begin to blink,
I think they laugh, or is it just me?
I pointed up, 'Look—there's a bear!'
But really, it's just a lost old chair!

The night rolls on with jokes and cheers,
We toast to friendship, sip on beers.
Each footprint left, a mark of glee,
Let's create more, just you and me!

Breezes Weaving Stories of Old

In the breeze, the tales unfold,
Of pirate ships and treasures bold.
I listened close, but all I heard,
Was someone snoring—ah, the absurd!

The palm trees sway and start to chat,
'Hey, look out! There goes a cat!'
With every gust, joy fills the air,
As seagulls circle and cavort without care.

The anchors weigh as stories soar,
While legends start to hit the shore.
I tried to catch one, made a fuss,
But all I caught was a pesky bus!

So let's share laughs like breezes blend,
Each silly tale, a perfect friend.
With stories tossed by waves of cheer,
We'll laugh aloud—happiest here!

www.ingramcontent.com/pod-product-compliance
Lightning Source LLC
Chambersburg PA
CBHW050317100526
44585CB00016BA/1567